A Red Fox Book

Published by Random House Children's Books
20 Vauxhall Bridge Road, London SW1V 2SA

A division of Random House UK Ltd
London Melbourne Sydney Auckland
Johannesburg and agencies throughout the world

First published in 1991 by Andersen Press Ltd

Red Fox edition 1993

Reprinted 1994

© Satoshi Kitamura 1991

The right of Satoshi Kitamura to be identified as the author and
illustrator of this work has been asserted by him in accordance
with the Copyright, Designs and Patents Act 1988.

Printed in Hong Kong

RANDOM HOUSE UK Limited Reg. No. 954009

ISBN 0 09 913951 0

From ACORN to ZOO

AND EVERYTHING IN BETWEEN IN ALPHABETICAL ORDER

SATOSHI KITAMURA

Red Fox

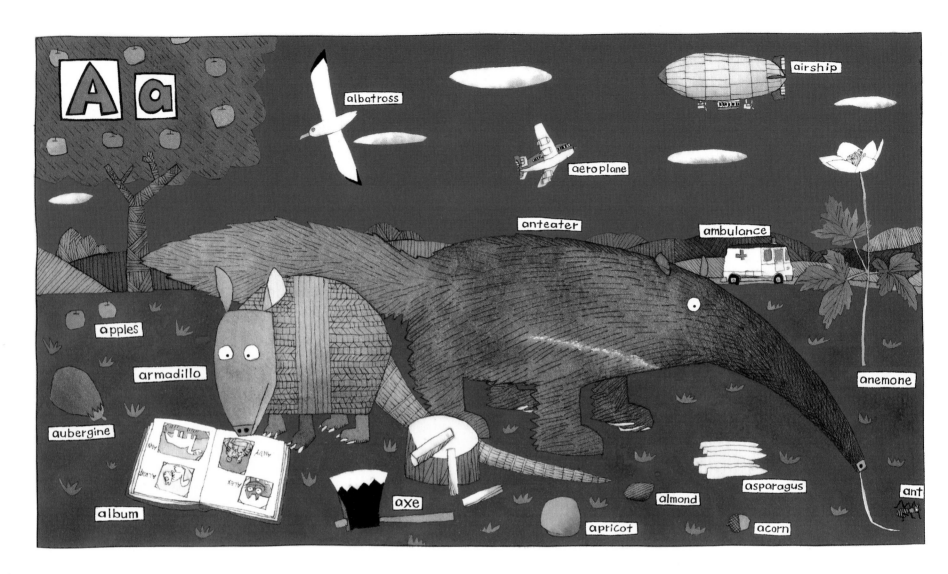

A a

albatross

airship

aeroplane

anteater

ambulance

apples

armadillo

anemone

aubergine

asparagus

ant

album

axe

almond

apricot

acorn

B b

brontosaurus
bus
bridge
bamboo
boat
bench
balloon
blackbird
bear
boy
box
book
bell
barrel
bottle
baby
basket
bread
butter
beetle
beaver
binoculars
ball
bat
bag
bicycle

C c

crow

clock

FEBRUARY
S M T W T F S
        1 2 3
4 5 6 7 8 9 10
11 12 13 14 15 16 17
18 19 20 21 22 23 24
25 26 27 28 29 30 31

calendar

Curtain

Cloud

Chimney

church

camel

cupboard

Cow

Candle

Cucumber

Crocus

Can

Cactus

Carrot

Cup

chair

Cabbage

cherry

clarinet

Cornet

Crayon

Cap

Cat

cage

Cobra

Chameleon

crocodile

Cockroach

D d

dove

daffodil

dolphin

dew-drop

dandelion

daisy

dog

duck

drum

dynamite

E e

egg

elm

eagle

earthworm

elephant

egret

eye

ear

easel

eider

envelope

eel

F f

fir

firework

flag

finch

fox

fire engine

fire

fruit

factory

fence

fork

frog

flask

fry.ing pan

fern

forget-me-not

fish

fan

feather

flute

G g

glider

giraffe

greenhouse

goggles

goat

garden

gate

girl

globe

goldfish

gloves

goose

guitar

grass

glass

ginger

garlic

grapes

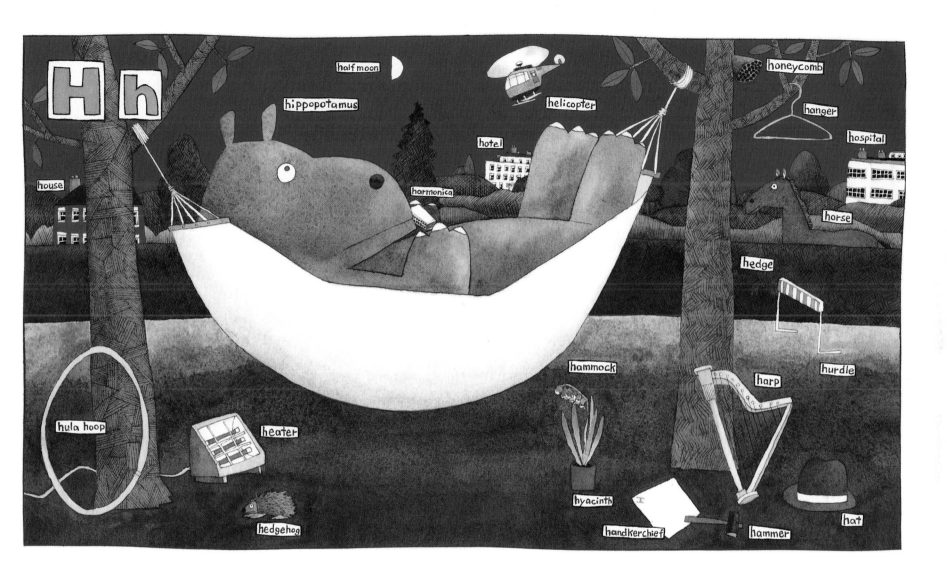

H h

half moon

hippopotamus

helicopter

honeycomb

hanger

hotel

hospital

house

harmonica

horse

hedge

hurdle

hammock

harp

hula hoop

heater

hyacinth

handkerchief

hammer

hat

hedgehog

iceberg

ibis

icicle

island

igloo

ice cream

iron

iris

ivory

iguana

ice

insects

ice skates

ink

J j

jungle

jet

jupiter

jewels

jay

jug

juice

jar

jam

jack-in-the-box

jelly

jaguar

jelly fish

jigsaw puzzle

L l

linnet
leaf
lightning
lighthouse
lamp-post
lantern
lily
lake
lawn
ladder
log
lamp
lollipop
lemon
lute
lettuce
letter
lion

Dear Mr Lion
Thank you very
much for the
lovely lute...

M m

moth
moon
marigold
mountain
mammoth
mop
magpie
microphone
music stand
monkey
matches
mushroom
mask
magnet
map
microscope
mantelpiece
money
mittens
mouse
mitt
milk
mug

observatory

overcoat

owl

oar

Octopus

ostrich

otter

Onion

okra

Orange

oboe

Ocarina

P p

pyramid

pipe
piggy bank
pitcher
pen
pencil

pine
picture book
piano

pelican
potatoes
Pheasant
penguin
pedals
pillow

page
pineapple
parcel

POST

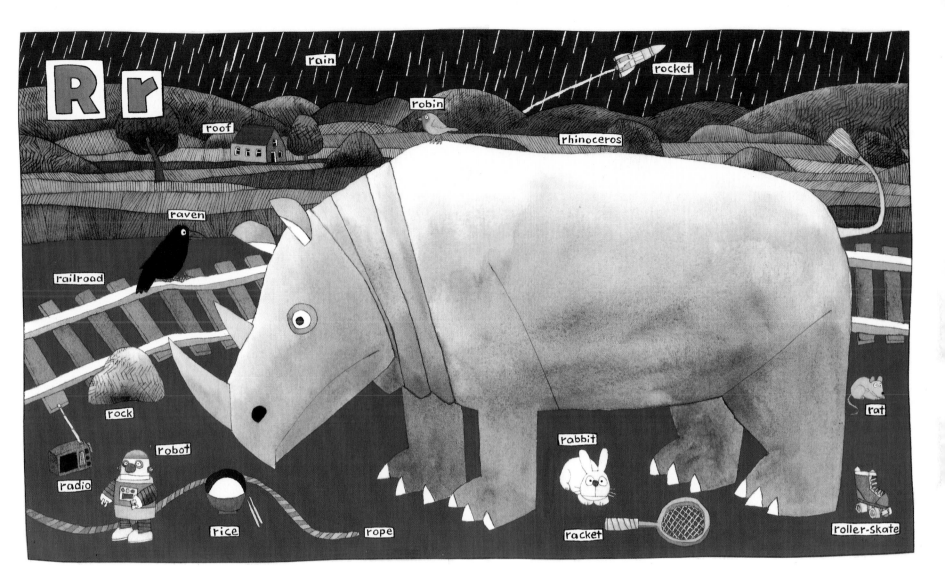

S s

sun

Sky

swallow

sea

Submarine

Shoes

seagull

socks

snorkel

Sunglasses

shark

Seahorse

Salmon

Sea anemone

Sponge   Sea urchin   starfish   seaweed   Squid

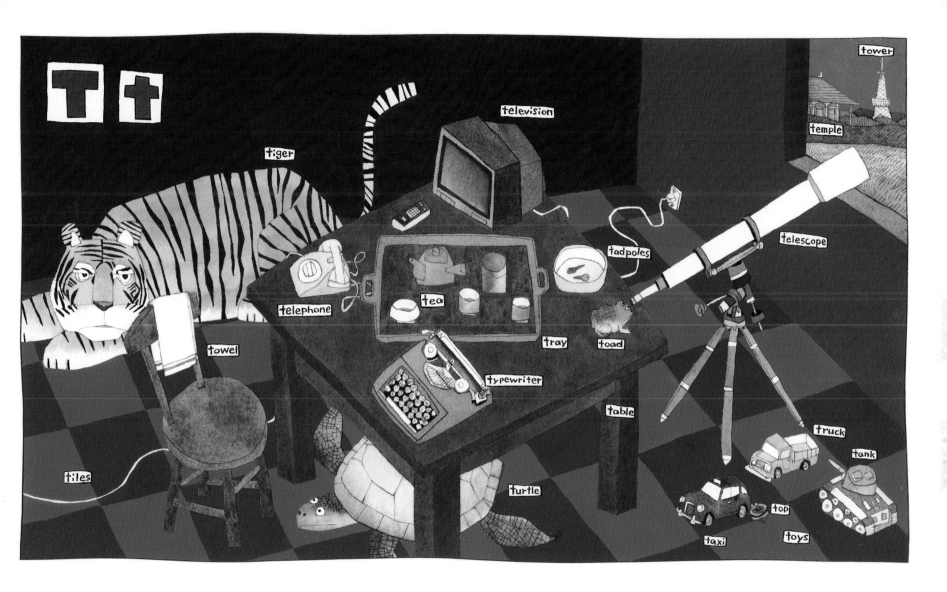

tower

television

temple

tiger

tadpoles

telescope

telephone

tea

tray

toad

towel

typewriter

table

truck

tank

tiles

turtle

top

taxi

toys

U u

umpire

unicorn

UFO

underwear

uniform

umbrella

ukulele

volcano

vine

V V

van

vulture

vacuum cleaner

viper

violet

violin

vegetables

vase

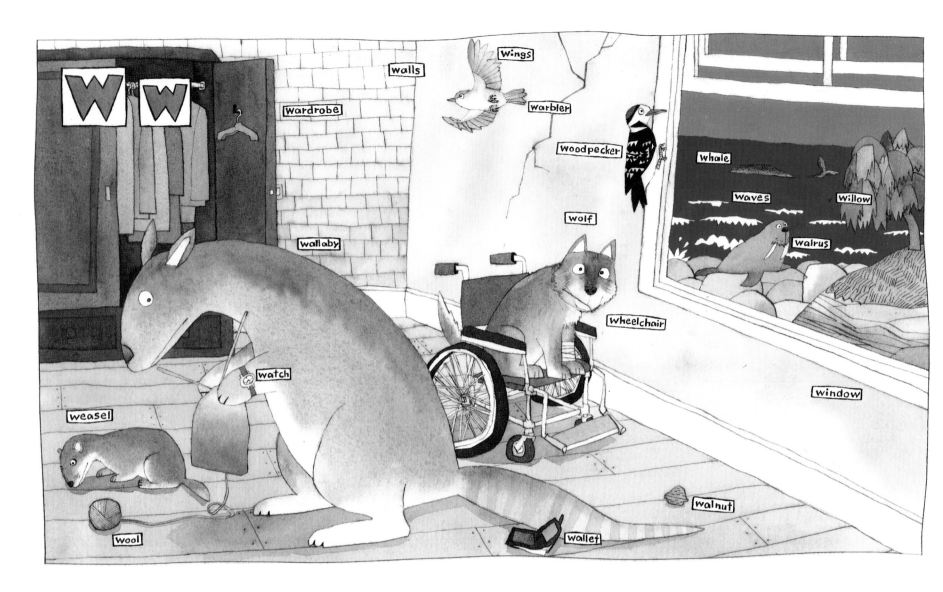

W W

wardrobe
walls
wings
warbler
woodpecker
whale
waves
willow
wallaby
walrus
wolf
watch
wheelchair
window
weasel
walnut
wool
wallet

abcdefghijklmnop
ABCDEFGHIJKLMN
WXYZabcdefghijk
WXYZABCDEFGHIJ
TUVWXYZabcdef
pqrstuvwxyzABC
MNOPQRSTUVW
ghijklmnopqrstuv
DEFGHIJKLMNOPQ

abcdefghijklmnopq
ZABCDEFGHIJKLMNO
WXYZabcdefghijkl
TUVWXYZabcdef
qrstuvwxyzABC
MNOPQRSTUVWX
ghijklmnopqrstuv
EFGHIJKLMNLOPQ

Some
bestselling Red Fox
picture books